D0500619

NORWAY

Beautiful country,
delicious food

Contents

The most Norwegian of the Norwegian!

With its vast distances and harsh climate, Norway is a land of extreme living conditions for both people and animals. The summers are short and hectic, the winters long and cold. Inevitably, this has influenced culinary development, and many Norwegian dishes and methods of food preservation may seem somewhat primitive or even peculiar nowadays.

Long before the Viking era, people were dependent on preserving absolutely everything they needed for the long winter: it was vital that nothing went to waste.

Many settlements in valleys and coastal areas were isolated for certain periods of the year, and so they developed their own traditions and methods of survival.

Rakfisk (partially fermented fish) is an example of one such method of preservation used for trout, salmon, herring and even shark. Originally, the fish was salted and then buried underground to undergo a fermentation process. *Rakfisk* is, and always has been, something you either love or hate. The strong smell that this dish can have was once described by Queen Kristina of Sweden's court physician as "the odour of excrement". Today *rakfisk* is an indispensable Christmas dish, and in many ways represents something quintessentially Norwegian.

Smalahove is another example of an ancient dish that still enjoys popularity with some people, while others regard it as almost vulgar and barbaric. *Smalahove* is sheep's head, salted, dried and then boiled; its keenest fans eat it with great enjoyment – eyes, ears and all! Can it be that the descendants of the Vikings are showing their true colours here?

These deceptively primitive dishes are actually most ingenious, and some, such as *gamalost* (aged cheese), were also regarded as a diuretic and an excellent aid to digestion, especially after over-indulgence. *Gamalost* gained its characteristic smell and taste after up to ten years of maturation, and was eaten by all classes of society. Today it is produced in modern factories, and is no longer matured for ten years, but we can easily imagine what a *gamalost* would look and smell like after such a long time.

No doubt the food could get monotonous, and it was probably for the sake of variety that new methods of preparing food were found. Lightly salted cod stored under seaweed on the shore to mature for a few days is one example from Finnmark, *lutefisk* (dried cod soaked in a lye solution) is another. Many people throughout the country ate these dishes in large quantities.

Cod belly stuffed with liver and barley meal, and *sursteik* (a roast marinated and tenderised in vinegar or sour milk) are other ways of making the most of ingredients, whilst more seasonal products such as gulls' eggs have always provided a little welcome variety in the north.

But in this field the Sami people, the aboriginal population of Norway, are unsurpassed. For thousands of years they have lived off and with nature in the extreme climate of Nordkalotten, the Nordic Northern Cape. Their lives are based on reindeer herding, hunting, fishing and farming, depending on which group they belong to. Reindeer Sami, Coast Sami, Lule Sami, Eastern Sami and Forest Sami comprise distinct groups, each with their own culture and culinary traditions.

The Forest Sami live for the most part in farming settlements, whereas the Reindeer Sami live nomadic lives following their herds of reindeer. Traditionally they lived in tents called «lavvoes» and their cooking was perfectly adapted to their way of life. Nothing went to waste: nutritious meals were prepared from all parts of the reindeer, such as boiled marrowbone, sausages made from entrails and brain, blood puddings and cheese made from reindeer milk. In the winter months the extreme cold acted as a freezer for meat, fish and milk.

Modern-day Norwegians do not have to worry about such things as storing and preserving food and securing access to ingredients. Norwegian eating habits are changing rapidly, and the menu in Norwegian households is showing signs of increasing foreign influence.

A taste of Norway

Impressive scenery, climatic contrasts and man's struggle against the powerful forces of nature. Norway, more than any other country, holds a special fascination for visitors, but its nature and climate are more than just the basis for memorable experiences, they have provided the ingredients for the development of a specifically Norwegian culinary tradition. Norway's long and varied coastline offers favourable living conditions for wild and farmed fish. The lengthy ripening process

 undergone by everything that grows in the Nordic summer lends an exquisite flavour to berries, fruit and vegetables, and the meat from animals which graze in lush, green summer pastures has an extra rich taste.

Norway is a modern, urbanised nation with booming oil and technology industries. Nevertheless it is clear that with only four million inhabitants spread over an area as large as Italy, unspoilt nature dominates the landscape.

Though eyebrows may be raised when Norwegian chefs win international prizes today, it's not the first time that foreigners have been impressed by Norwegian food. When the pope's personal envoy, Cardinal William of Sabina, came to Bergen to crown Håkon V in 1247, he was strongly prejudiced against Norwegian food and drink, having been forewarned. Nevertheless, in the speech he made at the banquet after the coronation, he was full of praise for the meal that he had been served. Unfortunately there is no historical record of the menu, but foreigners visiting Norway in the 18th and 19th centuries spoke highly of Norwegian salmon, fowl, game and strawberries with cream.

These dishes are frequently served to tourists today, and you don't even need to visit Norway to taste our salmon, as "Norwegian Salmon" has become a popular delicacy in many countries. Few people are aware that the export of salmon is a relatively recent industry, compared for instance with the export of stockfish, a form of dried cod.

Stockfish and lutefisk

Along the coast of Northern Norway, unsalted cod has been hung on poles and dried in the wind for more than a thousand years, and has been traded with other European countries in exchange for rare commodities such as wine, wheat and honey. The European traders called the fish stockfish, *stoccafisso* or *estocafix,* spelled in various ways, with a French cookery book manuscript from 1393 explaining how boiled *stofix* should be consumed with mustard or dipped in butter.

The fish must first be tenderised with a wooden hammer and then soaked in water for several hours. If lye is added to the water, the fish becomes especially soft and aromatic. The result of this treatment is the celebrated *lutefisk,* nowadays a Norwegian and Swedish delicacy as well as being closely connected with Norwegian and Swedish immigrants in particular areas of the US.

Flatbread and vegetables

It is true that many visitors in the past told of somewhat unfortunate encounters with Norwegian food. One Parisian lady offered the following description of Norwegian flatbread: «Norwegian bread is the shape and size of a plate, and has the same consistency.» Flatbread may not have been baked with equal skill everywhere, but this particular French lady was probably especially unlucky on that occasion 150 years ago. Today this crisp, wafer-thin bread is an important part of traditional Norwegian summer meals.

Many people complained about the lack of fresh meat and vegetables in the past. A Frenchman describing Norway declared: «It's a terrible country. There's nothing to eat. Believe me, sir, in all Bergen there are absolutely no vegetables or fresh meat to be had, no fresh fruit, no pears, no plums!»

His criticism was, presumably, due to the timing of his visit, as the choice of ingredients depended very much on the season. Had he visited Bergen in the autumn, he would have seen ships laden with apples from the fruit-growing districts along the Hardangerfjord.

Fruit and berries ripen slowly in the Norwegian climate, which gives them a unique flavour, and thanks to the cool climate and small number of insects, the use of pesticides is kept to a minimum. Today Norwegian-grown vegetables, fruit and berries such as Chinese leaf, apples, cherries and strawberries are in great demand in many countries thanks to their high quality. Norwegians have always grown tasty root vegetables, and modern chefs have become expert at combining these in new and exciting ways.

Salmon and bacalao

Almost all foreign visitors are impressed by Norwegian salmon and trout. Fresh fish is prepared in a number of different ways, but the most usual method is to poach it in large steaks. Restaurants now also offer a large variety of dishes made from other types of fish. Many of these are nothing to look at, but taste fantastic. For hundreds of years fishermen scorned these delicacies, throwing them back into the sea. One type of fish to be discarded in this manner was the catfish, even though Petter Dass, gourmet and poet from North Norway, insisted that one should not be put off by its appearance.

Another fish popular throughout the country is cod, which Norwegians prefer to eat as fresh as possible, and thanks to airfreight and modern methods of refrigerated transport other Europeans can also enjoy Norwegian cod fresh from the sea. Their ancestors were more familiar with dried varieties of cod, such as stockfish and clipfish, which are more popular abroad than in Norway. Clipfish is salted before being dried, and in the olden days it was laid out on bare rocks in dry summer weather, but today this process is carried out in thermostatically controlled drying rooms. Clipfish is exported to Portugal, Italy, Spain, South America and the Caribbean, where it is called bacalao and prepared in hundreds of different ways. In Norway it was simply poached, then served with boiled potatoes until the Spanish taught Norwegians to use olive oil and tomatoes. In recent years Norwegian chefs and gourmets have created exciting new dishes using this traditional ingredient.

Milk – the origin of all dishes

Gamalost (aged cheese) is one of several Norwegian cheeses made from boiling milk without adding the rennet normally used in European cheese production. The oldest Norwegian desserts were milk dishes, such as *gomme.* Lucky tourists may still come across this in some areas. Special dishes for weddings and christenings included sour cream porridge, a sweet, rich porridge made from thick sour cream. This is still an important part of a traditional Norwegian summer lunch, served with flatbread and cured meat.

Brown goat's cheese is perhaps one of the more peculiar sandwich fillings in Norway today. Foreigners generally think that it tastes of caramel, and are amazed that so many Norwegians have goat's cheese sandwiches in their packed lunches.

Many types of cheese made from goat's milk or cow's milk are exported, mainly to the US and Germany.

In the past, soured milk was used in the daily porridge which was usually prepared from barley or oats with water. This porridge has been highly valued by Norwegians throughout the ages.

Being readily available throughout the country, milk has played an important role in Norwegian cooking, and was sometimes added to meat dishes, too.

Milk was also used to make butter, an important commodity in the days of bartering. It was so exclusive that it was used to decorate the table at weddings, shaped into large pyramidal sculptures. The old-fashioned handcrafted wooden butter moulds used in the olden days are exhibited in folk museums today, and are superb examples of Norwegian craftsmanship.

Christmas fare

A traditional Christmas dinner normally consists of roast pork ribs in Eastern Norway, and cod, halibut or *lutefisk* in the coastal regions, although demographic shifts have partially erased these geographical distinctions. The time-honoured rice porridge is still served, but rarely for the main meal on Christmas Eve itself.

Nowadays more and more Norwegians choose turkey, although this is not so traditional here as in other countries. Other Christmas specialities include a number of sweet and savoury delicacies, such as pork head cheese (prepared in the Danish or German way rather than the French), mutton roll (a similar dish made from lamb) and many different types of marinated herring, sausages and meatballs. *Lutefisk* has become more and more popular as a dish for the pre-Christmas period. One of the most important features of Christmas fare is the many varieties of special Christmas biscuits, and the expression "all seven kinds" states clearly what the minimum aspiration should be for all ambitious housewives!

Cakes and gateaux also feature on the coffee table at Christmas. *Bløtkaker* (cream gateaux) are filled and covered with whipped cream and jam, whilst almond macaroon rings are piled up into high pyramids to produce the traditional *kransekake*.

Cured meat

The wide variety of cheeses and dairy products was a natural consequence of the fact that milk could not be kept fresh for very long. The long winters also made life extremely difficult for the population of Norway: the animals could only graze outside for a few short summer months.

Norwegians were therefore extremely dependent on dried, salted and pickled meat. Fresh meat was a rare luxury, as were cured meat and sausages. Norway may not have as much variety as Spain, for instance, but it does have a unique speciality called *fenalår* (cured leg of mutton). Fresh lamb, imbued with the fine, rich taste of fragrant summer pastures, has become popular both as a roast and in other dishes.

In the past, the best quality cuts of meat were reserved for the well-to-do, whilst to most people, fresh lamb generally meant the fattiest, poorest quality cuts, simmered with cabbage and whole black peppercorns to make *fårikål* (lamb and cabbage stew), regarded these days as a national dish

Pinnekjøtt (dried mutton ribs steamed over a rack of birch twigs), which originally came from Western Norway, has become a popular Christmas dish throughout the entire country. This delicious dish is about to be launched on the export market, hopefully with instructions for cooking and serving with mashed swede.

Beverages

Today Norway is primarily a coffee-drinking nation. Until the previous century, however, a mixture of water and sour whey known as *blande* was the everyday beverage for 90 per cent of the rural population.

Before coffee was introduced, those who could afford it drank beer, but on special occasions everyone drank homebrewed beer, a tradition going back to the Viking era, if not earlier. These days modern breweries have more or less taken over beer production, some of which also produce large quantities for export.

Norwegian cuisine

It is difficult to define Norwegian cuisine in the same way as is possible with French. Historically, Norway had no aristocratic and bourgeois classes affluent enough to develop culinary traditions, and apart from hotels the restaurant tradition was by and large restricted to a few mountain hostels.

Today, however, Norway can boast considerable diversity on the culinary front. Having travelled abroad, often on package tours, many people are eager to sample foreign food. It has become easier to get hold of the proper ingredients now that immigrants have opened grocery stores in Norwegian towns. Chinese restaurants no longer provide the only ethnic alternative: Mexican, Indian, Korean, Indonesian and Creole establishments all offer new and exciting gastronomic experiences.

As a reaction to mass-produced, standardised fast food, there is now a tendency to revert to the old Norwegian food traditions. People are once more leafing through Grandmother's recipe book, and a number of dishes with strong Norwegian roots, such as *rakaure* (partially fermented trout), *gamalost* (aged cheese) and *pinnekjøtt* (dried mutton ribs steamed over a rack of birch twigs), have regained popularity. The new generation of creative Norwegian chefs, who have proved themselves on a par with the culinary élite of the rest of Europe, focus on what is distinctively Norwegian. Using classical French methods, they create innovative menus which bring out the best in Norwegian ingredients. Some of these ingredients are among the finest in the world, and can be found in the kitchens of the greatest chefs all over the world.

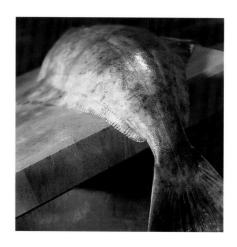

From the ocean and the fjord

With some of the world's richest fish stocks on our doorstep, fish has naturally been an important commodity both for Norwegian housewives and for the Norwegian economy throughout the ages. The excellent fresh fish has traditionally been prepared in a simple manner, to retain its natural flavour. Many dishes also arose from the need to preserve the fish, by drying, salting or smoking.

FISH

Barbecued trout in foil

Serves 4

Wash and dry the fish well.
Season with salt and pepper, and, if desired a little crushed garlic.
Place on a large, oiled piece of foil with diced vegetables.
Freshly chopped herbs enhance the flavour. Add a dash of
white wine if you have any. Wrap the foil into a parcel and
place directly on the barbecue. Cooking time will depend
on the size of the fish; a medium-sized fish usually takes about
20–30 minutes.

Salmon soup with saffron and mussels

Serves 4

300 g salmon fillet, skinned and boned
250 g mussels in their shells, or tinned mussels
200 ml dry white wine
2 dessertspoons butter/margarine
2 dessertspoons plain flour
800 ml mussel stock and fish stock/bouillon
200 ml cream
a few strands of saffron (1/2 g)
salt and white pepper

Method:
Scrub and rinse the mussels well and remove beard.
Boil in white wine until they open. Discard any mussels that
do not open. Strain and put the stock to one side. Make a roux
with the flour and butter/margarine and add the stock. Stir in the
cream and allow the soup to simmer for approximately 20 minutes. Add more stock/bouillon if the soup becomes
too thick. Add saffron and season with salt and white pepper.
Cut the salmon fillet into pieces, add to the stock and poach for
a few minutes. Rinse the mussels and add to the stock, saving
a few to use as garnish. Serve the soup with crusty white bread
and garlic butter or parsley butter.

Fish balls

Serves 3-4

500 g fillet of haddock, cod or a mixture of the two
2 teaspoons salt
1 dessertspoon potato flour
300–400 ml milk
1/4 teaspoon mace
herbs

Method:
Make sure all the ingredients are ice-cold. Cut the fish into small pieces. Place in a food processor with salt. Process to a firm mixture. Add milk gradually and mix well. Add potato flour, mace and herbs (such as finely chopped parsley, chives, thyme, basil or tarragon). You can also stir in onion, garlic, leek or peppers. This mixture can be used to make fishcakes, fish balls or fish loaf.

FISH BALLS
Bring approximately 500 ml fish bouillon to the boil in a saucepan. Shape the mixture into balls and lower into the stock. Allow to simmer for 5–10 minutes. The stock can be used in a sauce afterwards.

Poached clipfish with vegetables

Serves 4

900 g clipfish (salted, dried cod, ready soaked)
water
carrots
mange-tout
melted butter

Method:
Cut the fish into fairly large pieces and place in unsalted cold water in a saucepan. Bring the fish to the boil and remove any remaining skin and bones. Allow the fish to simmer very gently for approximately 5–10 minutes.

Serve clipfish immediately with carrots, mange-tout, boiled potatoes and melted butter. White sauce, creamed carrots and pieces of crispy bacon also go well with clipfish.

Herring with orange

Serves 4

approx. 800 g fillet of herring
finely grated rind of 1 orange
juice of 2 oranges
2 sprigs of fresh rosemary
1/2 teaspoon salt
1/2 teaspoon white pepper
50 g black olives, pitted
1 orange, thinly sliced
1 chicory

Method:
This dish can be prepared in a microwave or conventional oven.
Clean the herring fillets, removing any bones, and season lightly
with salt and pepper. Place in an ovenproof dish and sprinkle
with grated orange rind. Pour the orange juice over the fish and
add the black olives and rosemary. Allow to marinate for 2 hours.
Turn the fish in the marinade and microwave for 2–3 minutes.
Turn the fish over again and microwave for another 2–3 minutes.
Check that the fish is ready. Alternatively, bake in a conventional
oven for 10–12 minutes at 175°C.

Garnish with slices of orange and serve with rice and
chicory.

Mussels steamed in the white wine

1 kg live mussels
chopped fresh herbs, e.g. thyme and parsley
1–2 dessertspoons dry white wine
1 clove of garlic, chopped or crushed
1 onion, chopped

Method:
Clean the mussels and remove beard.
Discard any that do not close when tapped.
Fry the onion and garlic quickly in a little oil or butter.
Add the herbs, mussels and wine.
Cover and steam until the mussels have opened.

Serve with fresh bread.

Poached halibut

Serves 4

800 g halibut steaks or fillets
2 dessertspoons salt per litre water
1 teaspoon whole peppercorns

Method:
Wash and clean the halibut steaks or cut the halibut
fillets into serving portions.
Bring a wide saucepan of water to the boil with the seasoning added. Remove from the heat and place the halibut steaks in the
water. Bring to the boil and simmer very gently for 15 minutes,
but do not allow to boil.

Serve with boiled potatoes,
sour cream and cucumber salad.

CUCUMBER SALAD
200 g cucumbers
2 dessertspoons white vinegar
2 dessertspoons sugar
100 ml water
White pepper, salt and parsley

Method:
Cut the cucumber into wafer-thin slices; a cheese slicer can be
used for this. Mix the dressing and pour it over the cucumber.
Allow to marinate for a few hours before serving.

Trout with polenta cake

Serves 4

800 g trout fillet/butterfly/cutlet
salt & pepper
oil/margarine

Method:
Cut the trout fillet into 4–6 serving portions.
Season with salt and pepper. Fry/grill the fish in a little
margarine/oil over a medium heat until golden.

Serve with polenta cake, sun-dried tomatoes and tropical salsa.

POLENTA CAKE
200 ml coarse polenta
750 ml water
2 teaspoons salt

Method:
Place the ingredients in a saucepan and bring to the boil, stirring
until they take on the consistency of thick porridge. Place in a
greased mould, smooth the surface and allow to cool. Cut the
polenta cake into slices and fry with the fish.

Crab salad

Serves 4

meat from 1–2 crabs or approx. 350 g canned crabmeat
1 small tin of sliced mushrooms or approx. 50 g fresh mushrooms
1 small tin of asparagus pieces
1 small tin of pineapple chunks
3 tomatoes
1 red pepper
1 lettuce

Method:
Place a few lettuce leaves in a bowl.
Add layers of finely shredded lettuce, pineapple,
mushroom, asparagus and crabmeat. Pour sauce over and garnish
with tomato slices and pepper rings.

Serve with brown or white bread.

DRESSING
3 dessertspoons Normannaost (semi-soft blue cheese)
juice of 1/2 lemon
6 dessertspoons sour cream
3 dessertspoons pineapple juice
salt and pepper

Method:
Stir the lemon and pineapple juice into the cheese. Add sour
cream and flavour with herbs and a little sugar if required.

Marinade for shish kebabs

1 1/2 teaspoons salt
1/2 teaspoon pepper
2 teaspoons mustard
2 teaspoons Worcester sauce
1 teaspoon crushed thyme
a few drops of Tabasco
2 dessertspoons chilli sauce
2 teaspoons soy sauce

Method:
Mix all ingredients together to make the marinade.
Place the kebab ingredients or the prepared kebab in the marinade
for approximately 1 hour.

Meat for all occasions

In the past, meat was usually served on special occasions and feast days only. Nowadays dishes which were once reserved for weekends and celebrations have become everyday fare. Meat production in Norway is subject to stringent regulations, and most farms are small, which improves the animals' welfare. In the summer months, herds of sheep and goats are often put out to graze in the mountains, giving their meat a unique flavour.

MEAT

Lamb and cabbage stew

Lamb is very popular in Norway, especially in stews and casseroles, since it is tasty and easy to prepare. Lamb and cabbage stew is a national dish.

1.5 kg neck, leg or breast of lamb, cut into serving portions
1.5 kg cabbage
2 dessertspoons salt
1–2 dessertspoons plain flour
approx. 4 teaspoons whole black peppercorns
approx. 300 ml boiling water

Method:
Cut the cabbage into thick wedges. Cover the bottom of a large saucepan with meat, followed by a layer of cabbage, then meat, and so on. Sprinkle pepper, salt and flour between the layers. Pour the boiling water over. Bring to the boil and allow to simmer gently over a low heat until the meat is tender, for about 1–2 hours.

Lamb and cabbage stew should be served piping hot with boiled potatoes. Beer and aquavit are often served with lamb and cabbage stew.

Roast leg of lamb
Serves 4

1 leg of lamb, approx. 2.5 kg
2 dessertspoons salt
1 dessertspoon pepper
2–3 dessertspoons crushed rosemary
1 clove of garlic
2–3 carrots
1 large onion
water

Method:
Rub the salt, pepper, rosemary and finely chopped garlic into the joint. Stick a meat thermometer into the thickest part, taking care that it is not touching the bone. Place in a roasting pan with diced vegetables, mand roast in a pre-heated oven at 125°C.
After about an hour add a little boiling water. Take care that it does not boil dry during cooking. The joint will be rare when the thermometer shows 70°C. Leave it until it shows 80°C if you want it well done. Allow roughly 1 hour per kg of meat.
Let the joint rest for 15–20 minutes, and meanwhile prepare the gravy.

GRAVY
4 dessertspoons butter
5 dessertspoons plain flour
approx. 1 l of the roasting juices, and
a little red wine or bouillon if required

Method:
Make a roux of the butter and flour, over a gentle heat stirring continuously. When the roux is nut-brown, add the stock/wine. Let the gravy simmer for 10 minutes and season with salt and pepper.

Serve the roast lamb with boiled potatoes, vegetables and gravy.

Marinated sirloin steak

Use well tenderised sirloin. Marinated meat with bread makes a delicious starter or evening meal.

SEASONING MIXTURE
(for 600 g meat)
2 dessertspoons salt
1 dessertspoon sugar
1 teaspoon coarsely ground pepper
1 teaspoon dried basil

Method:
Trim the meat of any sinews, fat or membranes.
Rub the herb mixture well into the meat.
Place the meat in a dish and cover with cling film.
Refrigerate for 2–3 days, depending on the thickness of the fillet. Turn the meat a few times a day.
Will keep for about 1 week in the refrigerator.

Lamb carré marinated in beer

At the culinary Olympics in Frankfurt am Main in 1968, this rack of lamb was produced by the Norwegian Culinary Olympic team. On that occasion Norway took the gold medal, and was also awarded the USA's culinary Oscar, the Augie trophy.

Trim the rack of lamb of any sinews and surplus fat. Score the fat side in a criss-cross pattern. Rub with crushed rosemary, pepper and freshly crushed garlic. Cover the joint generously with Dijon mustard and placed in beer for about 4 hours. Remove the rack from the marinade and pat it dry before placing it in an oven pre-heated to approximately 300°C. When the rack is golden brown, reduce the heat to 90°C. Roasting time depends on how you like your lamb.

Serve with gravy made from the offcuts and bones, thickened with a little arrowroot.

Lightly blanch some fresh leaves of spinach, and toss them in clarified butter and a little freshly ground pepper, with a clove of garlic on the prongs of each fork to give the spinach a slight hint of garlic.

Place very thin slices of potato in layers in a small cast-iron dish with a little olive oil, with chopped parsley and paprika sprinkled between each layer. Bake in the oven until golden brown.

Marinating lamb or game in beer produces a fantastic combination of flavours. The taste of malt and barley provides the finishing touch and gives the meat a superb, fresh flavour.

Serve with chilled beer from the cellar!

Meatcakes with gravy and creamed cabbage

This dish is often known as "mother's meatcakes". In the past it was a matter of great pride for a new bride to be able to make meatcakes to match her mother-in-law's. Nowadays young couples probably share the cooking, but meatcakes have not gone out of fashion.

500 g mince
1 teaspoon salt
1 teaspoon freshly ground pepper
1 teaspoon ground ginger
1 dessertspoon potato flour
250 ml water
1 egg

Method:
Mix the mince with the seasoning and add the water a little at a time. Stir in the beaten egg. Form into fairly large shapes and brown them on either side in butter. Place in the gravy and let them simmer until cooked right through, for roughly 10 minutes. Season to taste.

GRAVY
2 1/2 dessertspoons butter
2 1/2 dessertspoons plain flour
500 ml stock

Method:
Make a roux with the butter and flour and brown slowly in a cast-iron saucepan. When the roux is nut-brown, add the stock and allow to simmer for 10 minutes.

CREAMED CABBAGE
approx. 1/2 kg cabbage, chopped
2 dessertspoons butter
4 dessertspoons plain flour
400 ml milk
1/2 teaspoon nutmeg
salt

Method:
Boil the cabbage for approximately 30 minutes in lightly salted water. Melt the butter in a saucepan and stir in the flour. Add the milk and bring to the boil, whisking constantly. Allow the sauce to simmer for 10 minutes. Turn the cabbage in the sauce and add salt and nutmeg to taste.

Roasted elk marinated in beer

Place a 1.5 kg tenderised, oven-ready elk joint in the marinade. Use plenty of beer so that the joint is immersed in the marinade. Leave this to stand in the refrigerator overnight. The next day, remove the joint from the marinade and pat it dry with kitchen towel. Brown the joint well in a cast-iron pan. Sprinkle lightly with salt, and place in the oven at approximately 100°C for roughly 1 1/2 hours. Take the joint out of the oven and let it stand in an ovenproof dish so that the juice can distribute itself through the meat, making the joint juicy and tender.
Pour the marinade into the pan and boil the stock until it is reduced by half, strain and season with salt and ground pepper. Whisk in a little crème fraîche to taste.

Serve the roast with wild mushrooms fried in butter, rowanberry jelly and small new potatoes.

MARINADE
1 l beer
2 bay leaves
fresh thyme
coarsely ground pepper
a few juniper berries
a coarsely chopped onion
a few sprigs of parsley

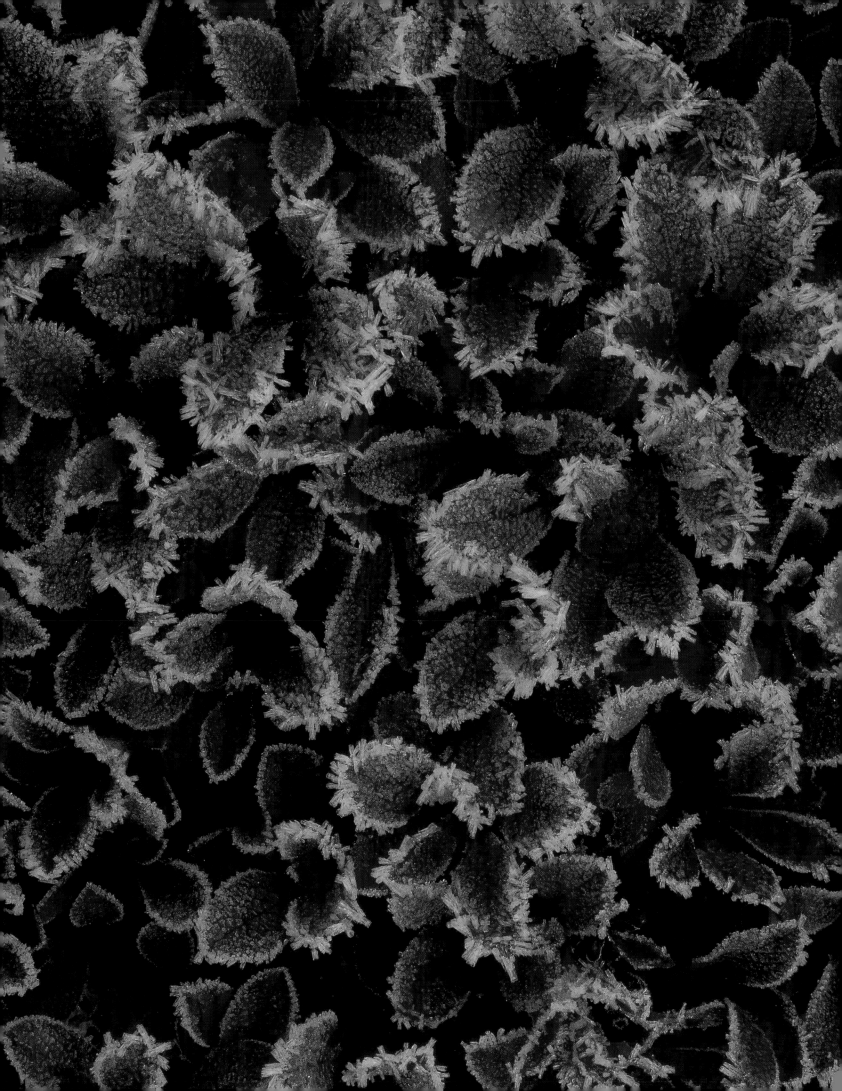

Norwegian cold buffet

The sumptuous cold buffet is a feature of hotels and restaurants all over Norway, as well as being a popular way of entertaining large numbers at home. Many of the dishes are delicious on their own as a starter or a light supper.

Smoked salmon, cured meat and a selection of marinated herring dishes are all indispensable parts of a Norwegian cold buffet.

COLD
BUFFET

Pickled herring

Use salted herring fillets with the skin removed. Soak in cold water for a few hours or overnight if they are very salty.

PICKLING LIQUID
200 ml vinegar
200 ml water
100 ml sugar

Method:
Boil the pickling liquid and allow to cool.
Cut the herring fillets into pieces and place in layers in a jar with onion rings, bay leaves, whole black peppercorns and mustard seeds. Pour the pickling liquid over and leave in the refrigerator for a few days.

Herring in tomato sauce

100 ml ketchup
100 ml soya oil
300–400 ml vinegar
2 dessertspoons sugar
3–4 salted herring, 6–8 fillets
1 onion
2 gherkins
1 bay leaf
a few cloves

Method:
Stir the ketchup, soya oil and vinegar together to make a smooth sauce. Add sugar to taste. Soak the herring. Rinse, wash and fillet the herring. Dry well and cut into very small pieces. Mix into the tomato sauce with finely chopped onion and gherkins. Mix well and add the bay leaf and cloves. Refrigerate for about a week.

Norwegian anchovies

1 kg brisling
120 g salt
160 g sugar
2 bay leaves
1 sachet of anchovy spices
approx. 50 ml vinegar
approx. 50 ml soya oil

Method:
The brisling should be fresh and not too small. Wash well in cold water. Mix the anchovy spices, salt and sugar together. Place a layer of this spice mixture in the bottom of a jar. Arrange the brisling head-to-tail, belly side up. Sprinkle a layer of spice mixture and a few drops of vinegar and oil between each layer of brisling. Place the bay leaves on top. Weight down lightly, and leave in a cool, dark place to mature. Turn the jar occasionally. Check that the brisling is immersed in the pickling liquid.
Ready in 3–4 weeks.

Trout fillet marinated in juniper

Use whole fillets with the skin on. To kill any bacteria it may be advisable to freeze the fillets and thaw them again before you begin marinating (it is safe to refreeze them afterwards).

For approx. 500 g fish you need:
300–400 ml sugar
100–200 ml salt
a few crushed juniper berries
freshly ground pepper
plenty of chopped dill
a dash of aquavit

Method:
Mix the sugar and salt, and rub into the fish.
Add pepper, juniper berries and dill. Place the fillets with their fleshy sides against each other. Make sure that the fish is well covered with dill both inside and out.
Weight down lightly and refrigerate. Turn a few times a day. Leave for 2–3 days, and towards the end of this time sprinkle a dash of aquavit over the fleshy sides.

Slice thinly and serve with mustard sauce.

Cheese board

A cheese board is an essential element of the Norwegian cold buffet. Choose a selection of cheeses and garnish with radishes, grapes, pears, celery and pepper rings.

Pickled salmon

Delicious as a starter or snack

1 kg salmon, skinned and boned
200 g onion
50 g salt

PICKLING LIQUID
1 litre water
600 ml white vinegar
750 g sugar
1 part white pepper
1 part cloves
1 part mustard seed
1 part bay leaves

Method:
Mix all ingredients for the pickling liquid in a saucepan. Bring to the boil, then allow to cool. The salmon should be filleted, skinned and boned. All fat should be cut away. Salt the salmon and leave for about 2 hours. Scrape off the salt. Cut the salmon into cubes, and slice the onion. Place the salmon cubes and onion slices in layers. Pour the pickling liquid carefully over the cubes of salmon and allow to marinate.

Buns

1/2 l strong white flour
250 ml tepid milk
50 g melted butter
300–400 ml sugar
1/2 teaspoon cardamom seeds
30 g yeast
1/4 teaspoon salt

Method:
Mix the dry ingredients in a bowl. Stir the yeast into the tepid milk and melted butter. Mix the liquid with the dry ingredients to form a pliable dough.
Cover and place in a warm place to rise. When it has doubled in size, knead well and roll out into small balls. Prove for 25 minutes, glaze with beaten egg and bake at 225°C for approximately 10 minutes until golden. Raisins and candied peel can be mixed into the dough.

White bread

500 ml tepid milk
1 dessertspoon melted butter
1/2 teaspoon salt
30 g yeast
approx. 750 g strong white flour

Method:
Sift the flour and salt together. Stir the yeast and melted butter into the milk and add to the flour. Knead the dough well and leave to rise. Knead the dough again, divide into portions and shape into loaves. These may be round, long or baked in a loaf tin. The bread should be left to prove for 1/2 hour and baked for approximately 45 minutes at 180°C.

Coarse rye bread

1.5 l milk or buttermilk
75 g yeast
1 kg coarse rye flour
1 kg strong flour
2 teaspoons salt

Method:
Add the tepid milk to the flour and salt and knead the dough well. Leave to rise until almost doubled in size. Knead again and divide into 3 portions.
Shape these into long loaves and place on a baking tray. Score the top and allow to prove for 45 minutes.
Bake for approximately 1 hour at 180°C.

Sour cream porridge

1 litre thick sour cream
1/2 teaspoon salt
approx. 100 g plain flour

Method:
Simmer the sour cream in a covered saucepan for at least 15 minutes. Stir in the flour and continue simmering until butter separates on top. Skim off the butter and served it hot with the porridge. For a lighter porridge, add a little boiling milk.

Smoked salmon with scrambled egg

Smoked salmon is usually served with scrambled egg in Norway, and no cold buffet is complete without this.
Cut the salmon into thin slices and place on a dish with quite solid scrambled egg, served at room temperature.
Garnish with fresh dill or parsley.

Cured meat with sour cream

Smoked ham, cured lamb and cured sausages of many varieties have long been an important feature of Norwegian cuisine. These are accompanied by scrambled egg, sour cream and chilled potato salad, or sometimes simply sour cream and flatbread. Smoked ham is at its best in the summer. Served with boiled potatoes and other vegetables, it captures the very essence of a Scandinavian summer.

Christmas biscuits

SAND BISCUITS
100 g ground almonds
200 g butter
250 g self raising flour
1 egg
100 g sugar

Method:
Rub the butter into the flour. Add egg, almonds and sugar. When the dough is pliable, place in the refrigerator for an hour. Press the dough into well-greased small fluted patty tins, and bake for approximately 10 minutes at 175°C. Remove the biscuits carefully from the tins whilst still warm.

BERLIN GARLANDS
2 boiled egg yolks
2 raw egg yolks
125 g sugar
300 g self raising flour
250 g butter
egg white for glazing
coarse granulated sugar

Method:
Press the boiled egg yolks through a sieve into a mixing bowl, add the raw yolks and whisk well together with the sugar. Add the flour and softened butter alternately. Allow the dough to cool.
Roll into lots of small, thin sausages and form each one into a garland shape with the ends overlapping. Glaze with egg white and roll in the granulated sugar. Bake for about 10 minutes at 175°C until pale golden.

SYRUP SNAPS
250 g golden syrup
50 g sugar
200 ml milk
approx. 500 g plain flour
100 g potato flour
150–200 g butter
1 teaspoon pepper
1/2 teaspoon ginger
1/2 teaspoon ground cloves
1 teaspoon bicarbonate of soda
1 teaspoon hartshorn

Method:
Melt the golden syrup with the sugar.
Sieve the flour. Mix the spices and the bicarbonate of soda with a little of the flour. Mix this with the milk and butter alternately. Add flour until the dough is no longer sticky. Sprinkle a little flour on top of the dough, cover and leave overnight for the dough to stiffen. Roll out thinly and cut into diamond shapes. Place half a blanched almond on each biscuit and bake in a medium-hot oven.

GORO
175 ml whipping cream
1 egg
125 g sugar
175 g butter
175 g lard
2 teaspoons cardamom seeds
1 dessertspoon cognac
1 dessertspoon potato flour
approx. 500 g self raising flour

Method:
Whip the cream until it is stiff. Mix egg yolk and sugar to mousse consistency, then mix in the cream. Mix alternately with softened butter, softened lard and flour with spices. The lard should preferably have been used to cook doughnuts beforehand. It is important to distribute the fat evenly, because lumps of fat will cause holes in the biscuits. The dough should be prepared the day before it is required. Roll out thinly and cut out shapes. Put them in a cold place and cook until golden brown in a special Goro iron, a tool for making flat biscuits with patterns.

Pinnekjøtt

(Dried mutton ribs steamed over a rack of birch twigs)

Pinnekjøtt was once a well-kept secret in the valleys and fjords of Western Norway and Trøndelag, but this hearty dish with its authentic flavour has now become popular throughout Norway.
Pinnekjøtt contains a lot of bone and fat, so you should allow 1/2 kg per person for a main meal.
Divide into chops by cutting along the ribs and soak in water overnight. Place a metal rack, or better still de-barked birch twigs arranged in a criss-cross pattern to form a rack, in the bottom of a saucepan. Fill with water to the level of the rack and place the meat on top. Bring the liquid to the boil and steam the meat until it is tender (approximately 2 hours). Top up the water as necessary. Some people like to brown the ribs under the grill for a few minutes before serving.

In Norway, pinnekjøtt is served on heated plates with sausages, boiled potatoes, mashed swede, gravy and mustard or mountain cranberry sauce.

MASHED SWEDE
approx. 1 kg chopped swede
Boil the swede gently in lightly salted water. Drain and mash. Add salt, pepper and meat stock to taste.

Cristmas rib of pork

Score the rind of the rib joint in a diamond pattern, and rub well with salt and freshly ground pepper, preferably 1–2 days before it is to be cooked.
Place the joint in a roasting tin and pour approximately 200 ml water into the bottom of the tin. Cover with foil and place in an oven preheated to 230°C, for approximately 30 minutes.
Remove the foil and turn down the heat to roughly 200°C.
Put the tin back in the oven and continue roasting for another 30 minutes. If the rind has not crackled by the end of the cooking time, place the tin on a higher oven shelf and turn the temperature up to 250°C.
Allow to rest for at least 20 minutes before carving.

Christmas ribs are traditionally served with boiled potatoes, gravy, Norwegian-style sauerkraut, sausagemeat patties, Christmas sausages, apples and prunes.

Delicious lutefisk feast for four

Serves 4

3 kg lutefisk
2–3 dessertspoons salt
1–2 packs of instant creamed peas
or dried peas
approx. 600 g potatoes
200 g bacon
coarsely ground pepper

Method:
We recommend roasting the lutefisk without liquid. Heat the oven to 200ºC. Place the fish skin side down in a roasting tin or oven-proof dish. Sprinkle with salt. Cover with a lid or foil. Roast for approximately 40 minutes at 200ºC. Dice the bacon and fry over a gentle heat so that the fat melts and the bacon becomes crispy.

CREAMED PEAS
300 ml dried peas
water
100 ml milk
1 dessertspoon plain flour
1 teaspoon salt

Method:
Soak the peas in water overnight. Cover with fresh water and boil until soft. Make a roux with milk and flour. Stir the peas into the roux and cook for 5–6 minutes. Add salt to taste.

Serve lutefisk piping hot on heated plates with creamed peas, boiled potatoes and bacon fat with crispy diced bacon. Have rock salt, pepper mill and mustard on the table.

Suggested beverages:
Chilled beer, and if you like, aquavit. Alternatively low-alcohol beer, non-alcoholic beer or mineral water, unless you are one of those people who prefer fermented kefir milk with their lutefisk.

Rice porridge

200 ml pudding rice
400 ml water
approx. 1 litre boiling milk
1 teaspoon salt

Method:
Rinse the rice in cold water. Bring water to the boil in a heavy-base saucepan. Add the rice and stir to prevent lumps from forming. Put the lid on the saucepan and simmer over gentle heat until most of the water has been absorbed.
Add the boiling milk. Replace the lid and continue simmering, stirring occasionally.
The porridge will be ready in about an hour, depending on the rice grains. Add salt before serving.

Serve with a lump of butter on top, sugar and cinnamon.

Sweet temptations

A well composed meal should end with something sweet. The following section contains recipes for cakes, yeast cookery and desserts. Norwegian fruit and berries have an exceptionally good flavour because they ripen gently in the cool, bright summers.

DESSERTS

Waffles

200 ml plain flour
1 teaspoon baking powder
1/4 teaspoon salt
1/2 teaspoon cardamom seeds
1 dessertspoon sugar
3 eggs
100 g melted butter
200 ml milk
100 ml cream

Method:
Mix the dry ingredients in a mixing bowl. Add eggs, cream, milk and butter and mix to a smooth batter. Leave to stand for 30 minutes. Cook the waffles in a waffle iron and cool on a cooling rack.

Serve with jam, butter, sour cream or goat's cheese.

Pancakes

300 ml milk
200 ml plain flour
2 eggs
1/2 teaspoon salt
2–3 dessertspoons melted butter

Method:
Mix to form a smooth batter, adding the butter last. Leave for 30 minutes before frying thin pancakes.

Serve with jam or sugar.

Gingerbread biscuits

250 g sugar
200 ml golden syrup
1 dessertspoon cinnamon
1/2 dessertspoon ginger
1/4 dessertspoon ground cloves
250 g butter
1 dessertspoon bicarbonate of soda
2 eggs
650–800 g flour

Method:
Bring sugar, syrup and spices to the boil. Add bicarbonate of soda and pour immediately over the butter in a separate bowl. Stir until the butter has completely melted and the mixture has cooled. Beat the eggs and stir them into the butter mixture. Finally add the flour a little at a time, working it in well. Leave the dough in the refrigerator for a few hours.
Roll the dough out and cut into gingerbread shapes or a gingerbread house.
Bake at approximately 175°C.

The gingerbread biscuits can be decorate with glacé icing.

Baked apples with vanilla sauce

Use large, good-quality apples.
Remove the core and fill with a mixture of butter, sugar and cinnamon. Place in an ovenproof dish and bake in the oven at 180°C until soft.

Serve with hot vanilla sauce.

VANILLA SAUCE
1/2 litre boiling milk
the seeds from a vanilla pod
150 g sugar
5 egg yolks

Method:
Mix the egg yolks and sugar in a thick-bottomed saucepan. Carefully pour in the boiling milk. Add the vanilla. If the sauce is not thick enough, heat gently until it thickens.
N.B. Do not allow the sauce to boil!

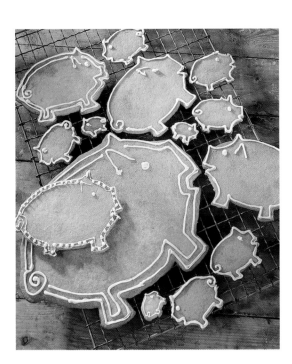

Veiled maidens

2–3 dessertspoons butter
200–300 ml sweet rusk crumbs
2–3 dessertspoons sugar
300 ml apple purée
300 ml whipped cream

Method:
Melt the butter in a frying pan. Add the rusk crumbs and sugar
and fry until golden and crispy. Place layers of crumbs, apple purée
and cream in sundae dishes or glasses.
The top layer should always be cream, topped with a light sprinkling of crumbs.

Cloudberry cream

200 ml cloudberries
50–100 ml sugar
300 ml whipped cream

Method:
Mix the cloudberries with the sugar and fold carefully into the
whipped cream.

Serve in individual sundae dishes or a large glass bowl.

Cream gateau

This is the cake that Norwegians serve on special occasions, particularly on 17th May, our national day.

SPONGE
4 eggs
100 g sugar
100 g plain flour
1 teaspoon baking powder

FILLING
200 ml raspberry jam
400 g tinned peaches
500 ml vanilla cream (half and half whipped cream and custard)
300 ml whipped cream
1 dessertspoon sugar
fruit/berries to decorate

Method:
Mix the eggs and sugar to mousse consistency. Sieve the flour and baking powder together, and fold in carefully.
Pour into a greased 22 cm cake tin and bake at approximately 180°C.
When cool, slice into 3 layers, sprinkling each layer with juice from the tinned peaches.
Cover the two bottom layers with jam, slices of peach and vanilla cream. Place the third layer on top and cover the top and sides of the cake with whipped cream. Decorate with fruit or berries.

Kransekake

(Almond macaroon cake)

Kransekake is our celebration cake, decorated to suit the occasion, an essential centrepiece at Christmas, confirmations and weddings. It is easiest to bake using special kransekake tins, but it is also possible to pipe rings of increasing size on baking paper. (Draw the rings on the paper first). The smallest ring should have a diameter of roughly 6.5 cm, and the size increases by 1 cm for each ring.

CAKE MIXTURE
250 g unblanched almonds
250 g blanched almonds
500 g icing sugar
3 egg whites

ICING
100 g icing sugar
1 egg white

Method:
The almonds must be completely dry before being ground. They must be ground twice, the first time on their own, and the second time with the icing sugar. Add the egg white to make a firm dough. Preheat the oven to 200°C. Over a low heat, knead the dough until it is almost too hot to touch. Pipe into the well-greased tins. Bake until dry and firm on the outside and soft inside, roughly 15–20 minutes. Allow the rings to cool a little before removing from the tins. Mix the icing sugar and egg white to form a thick icing. Pipe a zigzag pattern of icing on each ring and then stack the rings in a pyramid. Finally, decorate with sweets, flag etc.

Stressed cooks all in white

We joined four of Norway's top chefs at a training session in preparation for the prestigious Bocuse d'Or International Culinary Competition. 200 people in evening dress were seated in Gamle Logen banqueting hall in Oslo, waiting to be served a six-course meal.

Three waiters are standing at the end of the corridor, with the doors open. It is bitterly cold outside but they need a last smoke. They'll soon be bustling around the Gamle Logen banqueting hall. All 200 hungry dinner guests must be fed. This is the last training session before the Norwegian final which will decide who is to represent the nation of meatcake-eaters in their pursuit of the gold trophy.

«The selection of Norway's candidate for the Bocuse d'Or in Lyons will take place on 5 March, when six Norwegian finalists will contest the right to be Norway's sole representative in France. But we're all friends in this profession and we cooperate well. That's why we've joined forces this evening to create this sumptuous feast, working as a team,» explains Bent Stiansen, head chef, source of inspiration, organiser and winner of the 1993 Gold Bocuse Trophy.

The waiters stub out their cigarettes and shut the doors. Together we ascend the staircase to the banqueting hall. The waiters will be rushed off their feet for the next four hours, and we are going to be flies on the kitchen wall. Let's hope there won't be any flies in the soup!

Below the chandeliers in the magnificent hall, we hear sounds of rumbling, mumbling and grumbling. Not in the stomach region, but from deep bass voices. The Guldberg Male Voice Choir is entertaining the gathering, some of whom are dressed in evening dress, and many in white tie. Nobody is drumming with the silver cutlery or throwing the crystal out in the cold Oslo winter evening. For the art of cooking and serving at this level is a matter of precision.

«It's vital that we meet this deadline. People mustn't be kept waiting for their meal – it must arrive on time, not twenty or thirty minutes late,» says Bent Stiansen, who is jointly in charge with Eivind Hellstrøm, another renowned chef. More pepper. More olive oil. Can you, and you, take the butter in? Is the bread already in there? Can the starter be taken in yet? No?

Four finalists and 16 apprentices are rushing around in a sweat, preparing the banquet. Diagnosis: banquet chef's frenzy.

«Well, we're way behind schedule so far,» jokes finalist Jørn Lie to Eivind Hellstrøm. No problem there, for Lie's starter of salad with king crab terrine with coriander and tomato is already arranged on the plates. The waiters chew mints and glide around as only waiters can, as 8pm approaches and the white wine is ready to pour out. Lars Bermen would also like to go to Lyons to show the great gourmet Paul Bocuse what he can do. Lars is responsible for the evening's second course: shellfish galette on celeriac with apricot-ginger butter and ruccula. Is that a great delicacy?

«Doesn't taste of anything much,» says Bermen. What?!! We suspect a gastronomic scoop: «Championship

chef condemned at the first course!» But no, this is typi-
cal chefs' humour. Kitchen humour is always rough and
ready, you'd hardly credit it. «There are often quite
tough comments in the kitchen, although we never joke
about the food. Street humour,» says Bent Stiansen,
while the guests in the banqueting hall chew steadily
and politely. Grilled cod with garlic purée and sauce, a
creation by Charles Tjessem – delicious.

«Charles isn't with us this evening, but he is also
one of the finalists. He's in London busy promoting
Norwegian food. Kristoffer Hovland couldn't be here
either. He's on leave from Fossheim Hotel and has gone
to the Winter Olympics in Nagano to cook for the
Norwegian Olympic Team,» Stiansen tells us, whilst
Terje Næss saddles up a flock of lamb. This is the main
course of the evening – fresh saddle of lamb, pommes
Paolo and herb sauce. Terje doesn't have time to talk to
us up there under the kitchen fans, but we can hear his
incantation about herbs, parsley, finely chopped red
onion and MASSES OF GARLIC. Mmmm, that cer-
tainly looks tasty, but unfortunately we filled up on hot
dogs with plenty of ketchup just before arriving!

Trond Moi on the other hand tucks in. He's not
using garlic in his dessert. Still he hopes the guests will

react favourably when they are served white chocolate
and Grand Marnier mousse with melon salad and vanilla and strawberry coulis.

«I'd like to be picked for the Bocuse d'Or , but it
will be tough. All the Norwegian finalists are good, real-
ly good,» says Trond.

© Scandinavian Film Group, a Media Holding asa publishing company

Karenslyst Allé 10, N-0278 Oslo
Tel.: (+47) 22 12 16 70
Fax: (+47) 22 12 95 41

Design: Unni Dahl, Kristiansund
Printing: PDC Tangen
Text: Ministry of Foreign Affairs
Translation: Berlitz AS - Translation Services

PHOTOGRAPHERS:

Samfoto:

Bård Løken: 2–3, 4–5, 10–11, 19, 21, 22–23, 24, 31–32, 46–47, 48, 49, 64, 65, 68, 69, 72–73, 80, 81, 82–83, 84, 85, 99, 100, 101, 104, 105, 116–117, 118, 119, 120–121.

Åsmund Lindal 4 upper.

Jørn Areklett More: 4 lower, 27, 66–67, 98.

Steve Halsetrønning: 8.

Espen Bratlie: 14.

Per Eide: 15, 18, 51 upper.

Pål Hermansen: 20, 54.

B Areklett/S Myhr: 35.

Hans Hvide Bang: 50.

Leif Rustand: 55.

Dag Røttereng: 102–103.

Bjarne Riesto/Camera: 9, 70, 71.

Lisa Westgaard/Double Trouble: 6–7, 12, 13, 17, 28–29, 30, 36–37, 38, 41, 42, 43, 51 lower, 52–53, 56, 58, 59, 60, 61, 62, 63, 74, 76, 77, 79, 86, 88, 89, 90, 91, 92, 93, 94, 95, 96, 97, 106–107, 108, 110, 111, 112, 113.

Bård Ek/Dagbladet: 114–115.

Espen Grønli: 44–45.

CAPTIONS FOR WHOLE-PAGE ILLUSTRATIONS:

Page 1. A few years ago it would have been perfectly normal to have a beer or two in the kitchen while cooking. Now the chefs are more serious, especially those competing fiercely to go to the Bocuse d'Or International Culinary Competition in Lyons. This week four of the six Norwegian finalists met at Gamle Logen in Oslo to train together. The photo shows dessert chef Trond Moi, with two capable assistants, tucking into Lars Barmen's starter.

Pages 2–3. Midnight sun, Andøya, Nordland.

Pages 4–5. Summer night in Nykvåg, Bø i Vesterålen, Nordland.

Pages 10–11. Wind-swept flowery meadow, Bleik, Andøya, Nordland.

Page 14. Tidemand and Gude's *Bridal Procession in Hardanger*, which was painted in five versions (1848–53). The first version is on exhibit at the National Gallery in Oslo.

Page 17. Trout fillet marinated in juniper berries.

Page 19. Winter day on the coast, Sandfjorden at Berlevåg on the Varanger peninsula, Finnmark.

Pages 22–23. View towards Fortun, Luster in Sogn og Fjordane.

Page 24. Fish drying on a rack. From Svolvær in Lofoten, Nordland. The unsalted fish dried in this way is usually cod, but may also be pollack, cusk, haddock and other types of fish.

Page 27. Fresh Norwegian strawberries.

Pages 28–29. Flatbread. Unleavened, thinly rolled-out bread, cooked on a griddle. Descriptions date back to the late 11th century. Baked from different types of flour, such as oat flour and barley flour, as well as from mixtures including rye, potato or pea flour.

Page 30. Clipfish (dried, salted cod).

Pages 32–33. Winter mood, Hamnøy, Lofoten.

Page 35. Cows at pasture, Jølle at Lista, Farsund.

Pages 36–37. Traditional Norwegian sour-milk cheese, with a distinctive smell and flavour. *Gamalost* (aged cheese) is believed to have been known in Iceland as far back as the 11th century and descriptions can be found in literature dating from the 18th century.

Page 38. *Lutefisk* – dish made from salted or unsalted dried fish. The fish is soaked in water which is changed twice daily for eight days. It is then placed in a solution of ash-lye, washing lye or caustic soda for two days, before being soaked once more in water, this time for roughly two days. 1 kg of dried fish makes approximately 5 kg of *lutefisk*.

Page 43. Trout with polenta cake.

Pages 46–47. Winter morning at Træna, North Nordland. View towards Trænstaven.

Page 51. Lofoten fishing: seasonal fishing for cod off the coast of the Lofoten Islands. The season lasts from January to April.

Pages 52–53. Mussels steamed in white wine.

Page 64. Summer landscape, Kjerringøy, Nordland.

Pages 66–67. Mountain cranberries growing among the rocks.

Pages 68–69. Meadow with hay drying on racks, Aurland, Sogn og Fjordane, and front of old storehouse at Grimdalstunet, Telemark.

Pages 72–73. Misty mood at Aurlandsfjorden, Sogn og Fjordane.

Page 81. Rock carvings at Hjemmeluftfeltet in Alta, Finnmark.

Pages 82–83. Autumn in Døråldalen, Rondane.

Pages 84–85. Winter evening in Jotunheimen.

Pages 102–103. Cloudberries. A bog plant in the rose family, grows to approximately 15 cm.

Pages 104–105. Fruit blossom at Sørfjorden in Hardanger.

Pages 106–107. Cloudberry cream.

Pages 116–117. Birch trees in lush valley near Ulvik in Hardanger.

Page 119. Mardalsfossen waterfall in Eikesdalen, Møre og Romsdal.

Page 121. Rainbow at Vikspollen on Vestvågøy, Lofoten.